The Ivy and the Holly

14 CONTEMPORARY CAROLS

MUSIC DEPARTMENT

OXFORD

UNIVERSITY PRESS

OXFORD
UNIVERSITY PRESS

Great Clarendon Street, Oxford OX2 6DP, England
198 Madison Avenue, New York, NY 10016, USA

Oxford University Press is a department of the University of Oxford.
It furthers the University's aim of excellence in research, scholarship,
and education by publishing worldwide

Oxford is a registered trade mark of Oxford University Press
in the UK and in certain other countries

First published 2008

1 3 5 7 9 10 8 6 4 2

ISBN 978-0-19-336180-5

Music and text origination by
Enigma Music Engraving Ltd., Amersham, Bucks.
Printed in Great Britain on acid-free paper by
Halstan & Co. Ltd., Amersham, Bucks.

Contents

Composers' notes

1. Kerry Andrew: The Contest of the Ivy and the Holly

This is an ancient English carol from, it is thought, the time of Henry IV. The more well-known carol 'The Holly and the Ivy', collected by Cecil Sharp, originates from this text. Holly and ivy, both hardy winter plants and symbols of hope and longevity, are traditional emblems of men and women respectively. I have occasionally altered the words to 'Nay, *Holly*, nay . . . let *Ivy* have the mastery . . .' so as to give the women a fair go! The piece should be sung robustly by the men and slightly more sweet-voiced by the women, until the end, where they should be evenly matched in vocal tone.

2. Basil Athanasiadis: Antiphon to Mary

'Antiphon to Mary' was composed at the request of *Choir & Organ* magazine. In this setting of Hildegard of Bingen's text two different musical cultures coexist: Baroque polyphony and Japanese heterophony. The melody lines, which in Baroque music would be pitched exactly, are made freer here by the use of expressive *glissandi*. The organ accompaniment, which is influenced by the Japanese *gagaku* (court music) and the sounds of the airy *shō* (mouth organ), eventually hovers over the vocal lines in clusters. Thus Western and Eastern perspectives are moulded to create a unified language both at a musical and aesthetic level.

3. Alan Bullard: And all the stars looked down

I wrote this carol over Christmas 2007, specially for this book. It sets a haunting and memorable poem by Chesterton, which was originally entitled 'A Christmas Carol'. In the first three verses the contrasts between the traditional manger scene and the real world outside suggested the use of two opposing voice-groups, while in the final verse the vision of Christ reaching out to the world implied a unified, homophonic texture. The metronome mark is approximate, and the carol may be sung a semitone higher if preferred.

4. Richard Causton: Cradle Song

This is a setting of the famous cradle song, *Balulalow*, attributed to the Scottish brothers James, John, and Robert Wedderburn, who were born in Dundee in the late 15th and early 16th century. The piece should be sung with a smooth *legato*, and the refrain with a rather dark quality. It can be performed either by mixed choir or by solo voices.

5. Bob Chilcott: The Shepherd's Carol

I wrote this carol in 2000 for Stephen Cleobury and the choir of King's College, Cambridge, for their BBC *Carols from King's* television broadcast. The service had a focus on the shepherds in the Christmas story, and the then Dean of King's, Dr George Pattison, had chosen a number of readings and poems for the service, of which the text for this carol was one. I wrote this piece with the glorious King's acoustic very much in mind. When Stephen Cleobury performs it he always holds the last chord for at least ten seconds, which I love!

6. Michael Finnissy: Telling

Christmas is a time to reflect not only on the infancy of Jesus, but on God's purpose in thus directing our Saviour's life and death. This carol was first sung by the choir of the Church of the Good Shepherd, Brighton, under the direction of Malcolm Kemp, in December 2007.

7. Gabriel Jackson: The Magi

When Harrow School asked me for an Epiphany piece, one of the stipulations was that it should have a part for a separate choir of tenors and basses who would be in a gallery at the back of the chapel. This gave rise to the idea of a processional, where Yeats's extraordinary poem is intercut with the words of the Magi (Matthew 2: 2) becoming ever more insistent as they approach the manger. Though the piece is performable with a single body of tenors and basses, if a separate group is available it can be very effective if they move physically closer to the listener with each entry.

8. Cecilia McDowall: Now may we singen

I was contacted by Michael Lock in 2006 and asked to write a carol for the Concord Singers. For this commission I chose the text of the 15th-century carol, 'Now may we singen', and set it in a linear style, spare in texture, in keeping with the words. Sadly, Michael died before he could hear the carol; it was performed in his memory at the Corn Exchange, Bedford, in December 2007, conducted by Mary Lock.

9. Terry Mann: Gabriel fram Hevene-King

The early English text, which tells the story of the Annunciation, is based on the earlier Latin song 'Angelus ad Virginem'. In this setting the scoring denotes four distinct entities: the narrator (lower voices), the Angel Gabriel (upper voices), Mary (upper voices with a more intricate alto part), and Mankind in the final prayer (all voices). This piece is written for SATB choir, where there are enough singers to split each part. It was recorded in 2008 by the Leeds University Liturgical Choir, director Bryan White, on the Sound-Recording label; the recording is available via the choir's website at http://www.leeds.ac.uk/music/lulc.

10. Joseph Phibbs: St Margaret's Carol

'St Margaret's Carol' was written in 2004 as a spontaneous response to the death of the prominent British aid worker Margaret Hassan (1945–2004). Hassan's work in Iraq brought relief to hundreds of families whose lives had been devastated by over a decade of sanctions, and it is to her memory that this carol is dedicated. The tempo marking ('Andante, ma non troppo') is to be taken as a guide only; a slower, or more lilting, tempo could be adopted. Each of the *ppp* Latin refrains (bars 19–22, 27–30, 38–40, and 44–8) should be 'placed' very slightly, to emphasize the change in character. The first performance took place in St Margaret's Church, Ipswich, at the 2004 Christmas Service, directed by John Parry.

11. Francis Pott: Mary's Carol

This setting requires considerable freedom and flexibility of tempo. Metronome markings are only very broadly indicative of relative movement or repose, though in general the music invites smooth transition, not abrupt contrast or dislocation. The strophic arrangement of Peter Dale's touching poem is respected, but successive verses are delineated by loose generic similarities between their musical openings rather than any literal repetition. Undue lingering between verses (bars 20–3, 47–8, 64, and 85–6) is discouraged. The choral parts in the final verse (from bar 87) should be extremely hushed.

12. John Rutter: Dormi, Jesu

The Latin text of 'Dormi, Jesu' is of late medieval origin, one of a number of lullaby texts on the theme of the Virgin cradling the infant Jesus. The poet Coleridge (according to *The New Oxford Book of Carols*) discovered the poem on 'a little print of the Virgin and Child in a small public house of a Catholic village' in Germany, and made an English translation which was published in 1811. In my setting, written for the 1998 Christmas Eve Festival of Nine Lessons and Carols at King's College, Cambridge, I have used its first verse to follow on from two Latin verses and refrains, in homage to the macaronic tradition long associated with the carol genre.

13. Howard Skempton: Rejoice, rejoice

The context of a commission is always influential. The Festival of Nine Lessons and Carols at Truro Cathedral dates back to 1880 and I was keen to acknowledge the character and form of this much-loved service in my setting. I found the text of 'Rejoice, rejoice' in a 1937 anthology of English religious verse and was struck by its freshness and liveliness. The setting is lilting but not without irregularities, and any account of it should be both spirited and controlled. 'Rejoice, rejoice' was recorded by Truro Cathedral Choir, directed by Robert Sharpe, on the Regent label.

14. Andrew Smith: Veni, redemptor gentium

This famous Advent hymn is perhaps best known in Martin Luther's adaptation 'Nun komm, der Heiden Heiland'. The older Gregorian melody, however, has quite a different character from its more recent metrical counterpart. To emphasize the contrast between plainchant and polyphony in this setting, verses 1 and 5 need to be sung freely with a great deal of sensitivity to the natural stresses of the words. This setting is suitable for Advent or Christmas, and may also be sung by male voices alone. First performed by Consortium Vocale Oslo, 'Veni, redemptor gentium' was recorded in 2007 by New York Polyphony (Avie AV2141).

Translations

This section contains translations and modern renditions of substantial sections of foreign or medieval text used in the carols. Where only a few words require clarification, these are glossed on the carol pages themselves.

Basil Athanasiadis: Antiphon to Mary
Hildegard of Bingen (1098–1179)

O frondens virga,
in tua nobilitate stans
sicut aurora procedit:
nunc gaude et laetare,
et nos debiles dignare
a mala consuetudine liberare
atque manum tuam porrige
ad erigendum nos.

O flowering rod,
standing in thy nobility
like as the dawn cometh forth;
now rejoice and be glad,
and deign to free us weak ones
from evil custom
and stretch forth thine hand
to lift us up.

Gabriel Jackson: The Magi
Matthew 2: 1–2

Ecce magi ab Oriente venerunt Jerosolymam, Dicentes, Ubi est Qui natus est Rex Judaeorum? Vidimus enim stellam Ejus in Oriente, et venimus adorare Eum.

Behold there came wise men from the East to Jerusalem, Saying, Where is He that is born King of the Jews? for we have seen His star in the East, and are come to worship Him.

Terry Mann: Gabriel fram Hevene-King
14th-cent. English

Gabriel fram Hevene-King sent to the Maide sweete,
broute hir blissful tiding and fair he gan hir greete:
'Heil be thu, ful of grace aright! For Godes Son, this Hevene-Light,
for mannes love wil man bicome
and take fles of thee, Maide bright,
manken free for to make of sen and devles might.'

Mildelich him gan andswere the milde Maide thane:
'Wichwise sold ich bere a child withute manne?'
Th'angel hir seid: 'Ne dred te nout; thurw th'Oligast sal been iwrout
this ilche thing warof tiding
ich bringe; al manken wurth ibout
thurw thine sweet childinge and ut of pine ibrout.'

Wan the Maiden understood and th'angels wordes herde,
mildelich, with milde mood, to th'angel hie andswerde:
'Ure Lords thewe maid iwis ich am, that heer aboven is;
anentis me fulfurthed be
thi sawe that ich, sith his wil is,
a maid, withute lawe, of moder, have the blis.'

Th'angel went awei mid that al ut of hire sighte;
hire womb arise gan thurw th'Oligastes mighte.
In hir wes Crist bilok anon, sooth God, sooth man in fles and bon,
and of hir fles ibore wes
at time, warthurw us kam good won;
he bout us ut of pine, and let hime for us slon.

Maiden-Moder makeles, of milche ful ibunde,
bid for us him that tee ches, at wam thu grace funde,
that he forgive us sen and wrake, and clene of evri gelt us make,
and heven-blis, wan ur time is
to sterve, us give, for thine sake,
him so heer for to serve that he us to him take.

Gabriel fram Hevene-King sent to the Maide sweete.

Gabriel from Heaven's King sent to the Maiden sweet,
brought her blissful tidings and greeted her courteously:
'Hail, truly full of grace! For God's Son, that light of heaven,
for love of man will become a man
and take flesh of thee, Maiden bright,
so as to free mankind from sin and the Devil's power.'

Then the gentle maiden gently answered him
'How should I bear a child without a man?'
The angel said to her: 'Fear nothing; it will be achieved through the Holy Ghost
this very thing of which I bring news;
all mankind will be redeemed
through thy sweet child-bearing, and freed from torment.'

When the Maiden understood and heard the angel's words
Gently, in a gentle spirit, she answered the angel:
'For sure I am the serving maid of Our Lord, who is above;
For my part let thy saying
Be fulfilled, that I, since it is his will,
a maid, outside the course of nature, have the joy of motherhood.'

With that, the angel departed quite out of her sight;
her womb began to swell through the Holy Ghost's power.
In her Christ was enclosed, very God, very man in flesh and bone,
and was born of her flesh
at the due time, whereby a goodly hope came to us;
he redeemed us out of torment, and let himself be slain for us.

Matchless maiden-mother, fully possessed by mercy,
Pray for us to him that chose thee, in whose eyes thou foundest grace,
that he may forgive us sin and punishment, and cleanse us of all guilt,
and give us the bliss of heaven, when it is our time
to die, for thy sake,
(and grant us) so to serve him here that he may take us to himself.

Gabriel, from Heaven's King sent to the maiden sweet.

Joseph Phibbs: St Margaret's Carol
Anon., 13th cent.

Jesu. Holy Mary, mother mild,
Mater salutaris,   Mother that bring salvation
Fairest flower of any field
Vere nuncuparis.   You are truly called
With Jesus Christ you were with child;
You drive me from my musings wild
Potente,   Powerfully
Which make me go to death, I know,
Repente.   Suddenly

Jesu. Levedi, flour of alle thing,   Jesu. Lady, flower of all things,
Rosa sine spina,   Rose without a thorn
Thu bere Jhesu hevene king,   Thou borest Jesus, heaven's king
Gratia divina;   By God's grace
Of alle thu berst the pris,   Of all (people) thou bearest the prize,
Levedi, quene of Parays   Lady, chosen queen
Electa,   of Paradise,
Mayde, milde Moder,   maiden, thou hast been made
es Effecta.   a gentle mother.

Verse 1 from *Medieval English Verse* (Penguin Classics, 1964). © Brian Stone, 1964.
Reproduced by permission.

John Rutter: Dormi, Jesu
Latin, origin unknown; trans. S. T. Coleridge (1772–1834)

Dormi, Jesu! mater ridet   Sleep, sweet baby! my cares beguiling:
Quae tam dulcem somnum videt,   Mother sits beside thee, smiling;
Dormi, Jesu blandule.   Sleep, my darling, tenderly.

Si non dormis, mater plorat   If thou sleep not, mother mourneth,
Inter fila cantans orat,   Singing as her wheel she turneth:
Blande, veni, somnule.   Come, soft slumber, balmily.

Andrew Smith: Veni, redemptor gentium
St Ambrose (340–97)

Veni, redemptor gentium,   Saviour of the nations, come,
Ostende partum Virginis;   recognized as the Virgin's child,
Miretur omne saeculum: so that the world marvels
Talis decet partus Deum.   that God ordained such a birth for Him.

Sit, Christe, rex piisime,   To Christ the most holy King
Tibi Patrique gloria   and to you the Father be glory,
Cum Spiritu Paraclito,   and with the Holy Spirit,
In sempiterna saecula. Amen.   world without end. Amen.

Translation © New York Polyphony. Reproduced by permission.

Liturgical table

Advent
Antiphon to Mary
Gabriel fram Hevene-King
St Margaret's Carol
Veni, redemptor gentium

Annunciation
Gabriel fram Hevene-King

Christmas
And all the stars looked down
Cradle Song
Dormi, Jesu
Now may we singen
Rejoice, rejoice
Telling
The Shepherd's Carol
Veni, redemptor gentium

Epiphany
Mary's Carol
The Magi

Many of the carols in this collection, and especially 'The Contest of the Ivy and the Holly' and 'Telling', are also suitable for singing at other times of year.

The Ivy and the Holly

1. The Contest of the Ivy and the Holly

Trad. English, adap.

KERRY ANDREW
(b. 1978)

(oo)_____ she is full__ sore__ a cold. mm_____

I - vy stands with-out the door, mm_____

(mm)_____

(stagger breathing)

mm_____

(mm)_____

S.

(mm)_____

A.

(mm)_____

SOLO or TENOR 1

T. 1

Nay, I - vy, nay,___ it shall not be I ¹wis;___ let Hol-ly have_ the

TUTTI or TENOR 2

T. 2

mm_____

B.

(mm)_____

mf

¹*wis* think

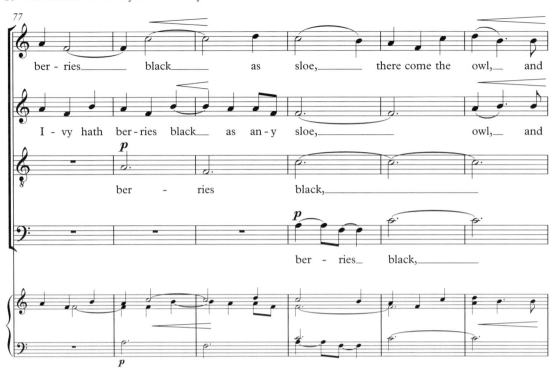

2. Antiphon to Mary

Hildegard of Bingen
(1098–1179)

BASIL ATHANASIADIS
(b. 1970)

See p. ix for a translation of this poem.

3. And all the stars looked down

Gilbert Keith Chesterton
(1874–1936)

ALAN BULLARD
(b. 1947)

This carol may be transposed up a semitone into E flat minor.

for David Wordsworth and the Addison Singers

4. Cradle Song

attrib. James, John, and Robert Wedderburn (*c.*1567)

RICHARD CAUSTON
(b. 1971)

*Basses, bars 25–6: the lower note may be omitted if sung by solo voices.

for Stephen Cleobury and the Choir of King's College, Cambridge

5. The Shepherd's Carol

Anon.

BOB CHILCOTT
(b. 1955)

Also available separately (ISBN 978–0–19–343296–3) and in *Bob Chilcott Carols: 9 carols for mixed voices* (ISBN 978–0–19–353233–5).

so we have come, La - dy, Our day's work done, Our

Our

S. love,___ our hopes, our - selves___ we give to your son.___

A. Love,___ our - selves___ La - dy,

T. love,___ our hopes, our - selves___ La - dy,

B.1 Love,___ our - selves___ La - dy,

B.2 Love,___ our - selves___ La - dy, La -

6. Telling

Anon., 16th cent.

MICHAEL FINNISSY
(b. 1946)

Variations in tempo and dynamics should subtly follow the sense of the words and the shape of the phrases; details are at the discretion of the performers and their director.

Commissioned by Harrow School

7. The Magi

Latin: Matthew 2: 1–2
English: W. B. Yeats (1865–1939)

GABRIEL JACKSON
(b. 1962)

First performed by the choirs of Harrow School, directed by David Woodcock, on 6 December 2006. *The Magi* is recorded by Tewkesbury Abbey Schola Cantorum, directed by Benjamin Nicholas, on Delphian DCD34047.

See p. ix for a translation of the Latin text.

*Bars 13–17, 30–4, 45–8, and 55–7 may be sung by a separate group of tenors and basses, at a distance from the main choir.

repeat *ad lib.*,
independently
of the barline

In their stiff, paint - ed clothes, the pale un - sa - tis-

- fied ones Ap-pear and dis-ap - pear in the

an-cient fa - ces___ like rain - beat - en stones, And all their helms of

an-cient fa - ces___ like rain - beat - en stones, And all their helms of

an-cient fa - ces___ like rain - beat - en stones, And all their helms of

an-cient fa - ces___ like rain - beat - en stones, And all their helms of

sil - - - ver ho-ver-ing side by side,___ And

sil - ver___ ho - ver - ing side by side,___ And

sil-ver ho - ver-ing side by side, And

sil - - - ver side by side, And

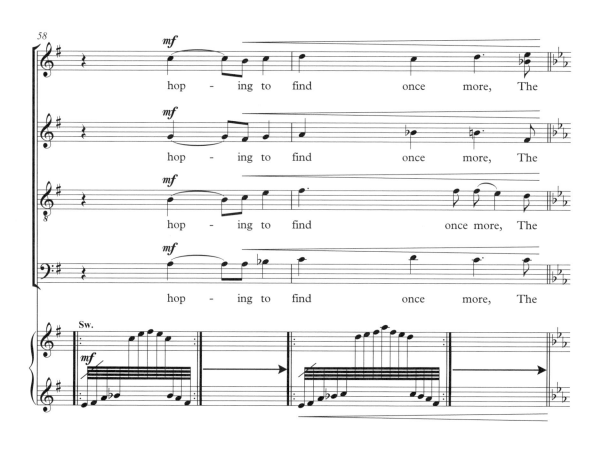

for Michael Lock
Commissioned by the Concord Singers

8. Now may we singen

15th-cent. English

CECILIA McDOWALL
(b. 1951)

[1] *ywrought* made
[2] *forlorn* lost, forsaken
[3] *forsooth ywis* in truth indeed

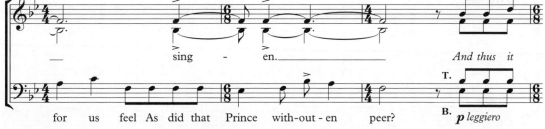

[4] *quod puer natus est nobis* because a boy is born to us

Be mer-cy asked and He be prayed, Who may de-serve the heav-en-ly

Be___ and He___ de-serve

sing - en.___

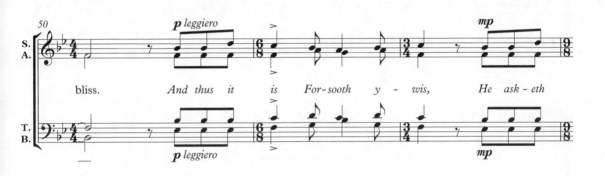

S. A.

bliss.   *And thus it is For-sooth y - wis, He ask - eth*

T. B.

p leggiero   *mp*

nought but that is His.   Now may we sing - en, now may we sing - en

mf

as it is.   *Quod pu - er na - tus est,___ na - tus est,___ quod__ pu - er,*

Quod pu - er na - tus est,___ na - tus,

for Stephen Bullamore and the choir of Waltham Abbey

9. Gabriel fram Hevene-King

14th-cent. English

TERRY MANN
(b. 1963)

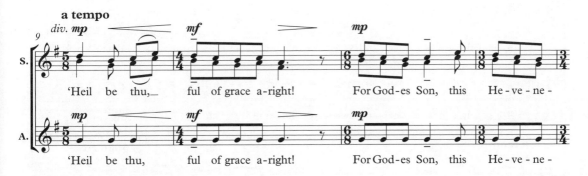

The three different pause symbols indicate three basic lengths: short (∧), normal (⌒), and long (⊓); the exact duration is left to the conductor's discretion.

Commas indicate a very small pause, as for a breath.

Pronunciation: generally, pronounce the 'e' of the ends of the words as 'er' (like modern German) where stressed in the setting; 'ee' is pronounced 'ay' (like modern Dutch). Thus 'Maide sweete' becomes 'Mai-d*er* sway-t*er*'.

See p. ix for a modern rendition of this poem.

mil-de-lich, with mil-de mood, to th'an-gel hie and - swer-de:

mil-de-lich, with mil-de mood, to th'an-gel hie and - swer - de:

S. 'U - re Lords the-we maid i - wis ich am, that heer a - bo-ven is; a -

A. 'U - re Lords the-we maid i - wis ich, that heer a - bo - ven is; a -

S. - nen - tis me ful - fur - thed be thi sawe that ich, sith his wil

A. - nen - tis ful - fur - thed be thi sawe that ich,

A. - nen - tis me ful - fur-thed be thi sawe that ich,

is, a maid, with-u-te la - we,

a maid, la - we, of mo - der, have the blis.'

maid, of mo - der, have the blis.'

maid, la - we,

C

a tempo poco rit.

T. Th'an-gel went a - wei mid that al ut of hi - re sigh - te;

B. Th'an-gel went a - wei mid that al ut of hi - re sigh - te;

*Keyboard reduction for rehearsal only.

Written for St Margaret's Church Choir, Ipswich, and dedicated to the memory
of the aid worker Margaret Hassan (1945–2004)

10. St Margaret's Carol

Anon., 13th cent.

JOSEPH PHIBBS
(b. 1974)

*The Processional (bars 1–6) is optional but is preferred, even when not literally processed. If processing, repeat bars 3–4 *ad lib.*
as required; if not, sing them twice.

†Sing 'Yaysu'.

See p. xi for a translation of the text.

Words (verse 1): from *Medieval English Verse*, translated with an introduction by Brian Stone (Penguin Classics, 1964). Copyright © Brian
Stone, 1964. Reproduced by permission of Penguin Books Ltd.
Music © Oxford University Press 2008. Photocopying this copyright material is ILLEGAL.

†Sing 'Yaysu'.

*Sing 'alle' as two syllables in bar 17.

in loving memory of my father-in-law,
Rear Admiral Bryan Straker, who died on Christmas Day 2007

11. Mary's Carol

Peter Dale
(b. 1938)

FRANCIS POTT
(b. 1957)

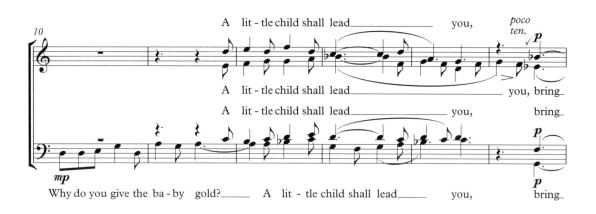

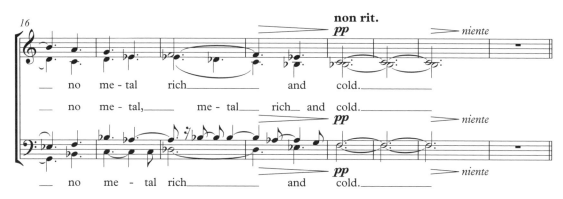

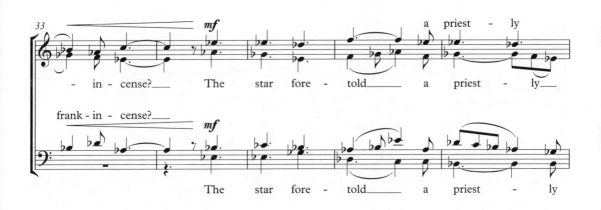

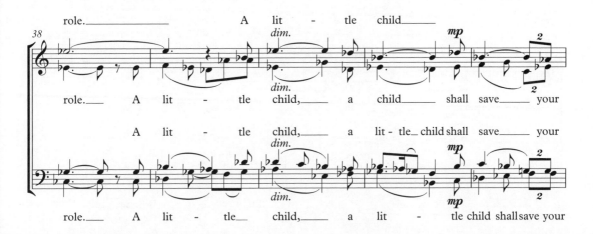

the earth,___

Sa - viour born to__ save__ the earth, our Way, our Way, our Truth, our Light,___

the earth,___

__ our Way,___ our Truth,___ our___ Light.___

SOPRANO SOLO *mp*   *poco ten.*

S. SOLO

Why do you give the__ ba - by__ gold?___

pp molto sostenuto, con tenerezza

S.
A.

Three gifts that far__ out - weigh__ all gold___

T.
B.

pp molto sostenuto, con tenerezza

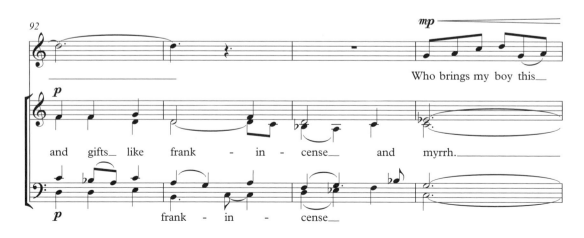

mp

Who brings my boy this__

p

and gifts__ like frank - in - cense__ and myrrh.___

p   frank - in - cense___

for Stephen Cleobury and the Choir of King's College, Cambridge

12. Dormi, Jesu

Words: Latin, origin unknown
English, S. T. Coleridge (1772–1834)

JOHN RUTTER
(b. 1945)

See p. xi for a translation of the Latin text.

Also available separately (ISBN 978–0–19–343241–3) and in *John Rutter Carols: 10 carols for mixed voices* (ISBN 978–0–19–353381–3).
The accompaniment is scored for strings, and is available on hire from the Publisher's Hire Library, or appropriate agent.

smil-ing; Sleep, my dar-ling, sleep, my dar-ling, ten- der- ly._

smil - ing; Sleep, my dar - ling,_ sleep, my dar - ling,_ ten - der- ly._

smil - ing; Sleep, my dar - ling, sleep, my dar - ling, ten - der- ly.

smil - ing; Sleep, my dar - ling, sleep, my dar - ling, ten - der- ly.

S. 1 Dor - mi, Je - su, dor - mi, Je - su, dor - mi, Je - su blan - du - le:

S. 2 Dor - mi, Je - su, dor - mi, Je - su, dor - mi, Je - su blan - du - le:

A. Dor - mi,_ dor - mi, dor - mi, Je - su blan - du - le:_

T. Dor - mi, dor - mi, Je - su,_ dor - mi, Je - su_ blan - du - le:

B. 1 Dor - mi, dor - mi, dor - mi, Je - su_ blan - du - le:

B. 2 Dor - mi, Je - su, dor - mi, Je - su, dor - mi, Je - su_ blan - du - le:

poco rall.

p

(*small notes optional*)

Commissioned for the 2007 Festival of Nine Lessons and Carols in Truro Cathedral
by the Precentor, Canon Perran Gay, in memory of his mother, Pamela

13. Rejoice, rejoice

Francis Kinwelmershe
(?1540–80)

HOWARD SKEMPTON
(b. 1947)

for New York Polyphony

14. Veni, redemptor gentium

St Ambrose (340–97)
vv. 2, 3, and 4 trans. William Morton Reynolds

Einsiedeln/Erfurt
arr. ANDREW SMITH (b. 1970)

See p. xi for a translation of the Latin text.

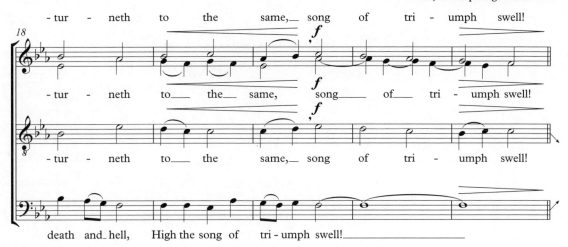

-tur - neth to the same, song of tri - umph swell!

-tur - neth to the same, song of tri - umph swell!

-tur - neth to the same, song of tri - umph swell!

death and hell, High the song of tri - umph swell!

S. A.

4. Bright-ly doth Thy man - ger shine, Glo - rious is its light div - ine.

T. B.

Let not sin o'er - cloud this light; Ev - er be our faith thus bright.

Freely

TUTTI *unis.*

mf

5. Sit, Chri - ste, rex pi - is - si - me, Ti - bi Pa - tri - que glo - ri - a

Cum Spi - ri - tu Pa - ra - cli - to, In sem - pi - ter - na sae - cu - la. A - men.